ICONIC GUITARS

2025 CALENDAR

I0624458

JANUARY 2025

SUNDAY	MONDAY	TUESDAY	WEDNESDAY	THURSDAY	FRIDAY	SATURDAY
29	30	31	1	2	3 John Paul Jones Born on this day 1946	4
5	6 Malcolm Young Born on this day 1953	7	8	9 Jimmy Page Born on this day 1944 Dave Matthews Born on this day 1969	10	11
12	13	14 Zakk Wylde Born on this day 1967 Dave Grohl Born on this day 1969	15	16	17	18
19	20	21	22	23	24	25
26 Eddie Van Halen Born on this day 1955.	27	28	29	30	31	1

FEBRUARY 2025

SUNDAY	MONDAY	TUESDAY	WEDNESDAY	THURSDAY	FRIDAY	SATURDAY
26	27	28	29	30	31	1
2	3	4	5	6	7 Wes Borland Born on this day 1975	8
9	10	11	12	13	14	15
16	17 Billie Joe Armstrong Born on this day 1972	18	19 Tony Iommi Born on this day 1948	20	21	22
23	24	25 George Harrison Born on this day 1943	26	27	28	1

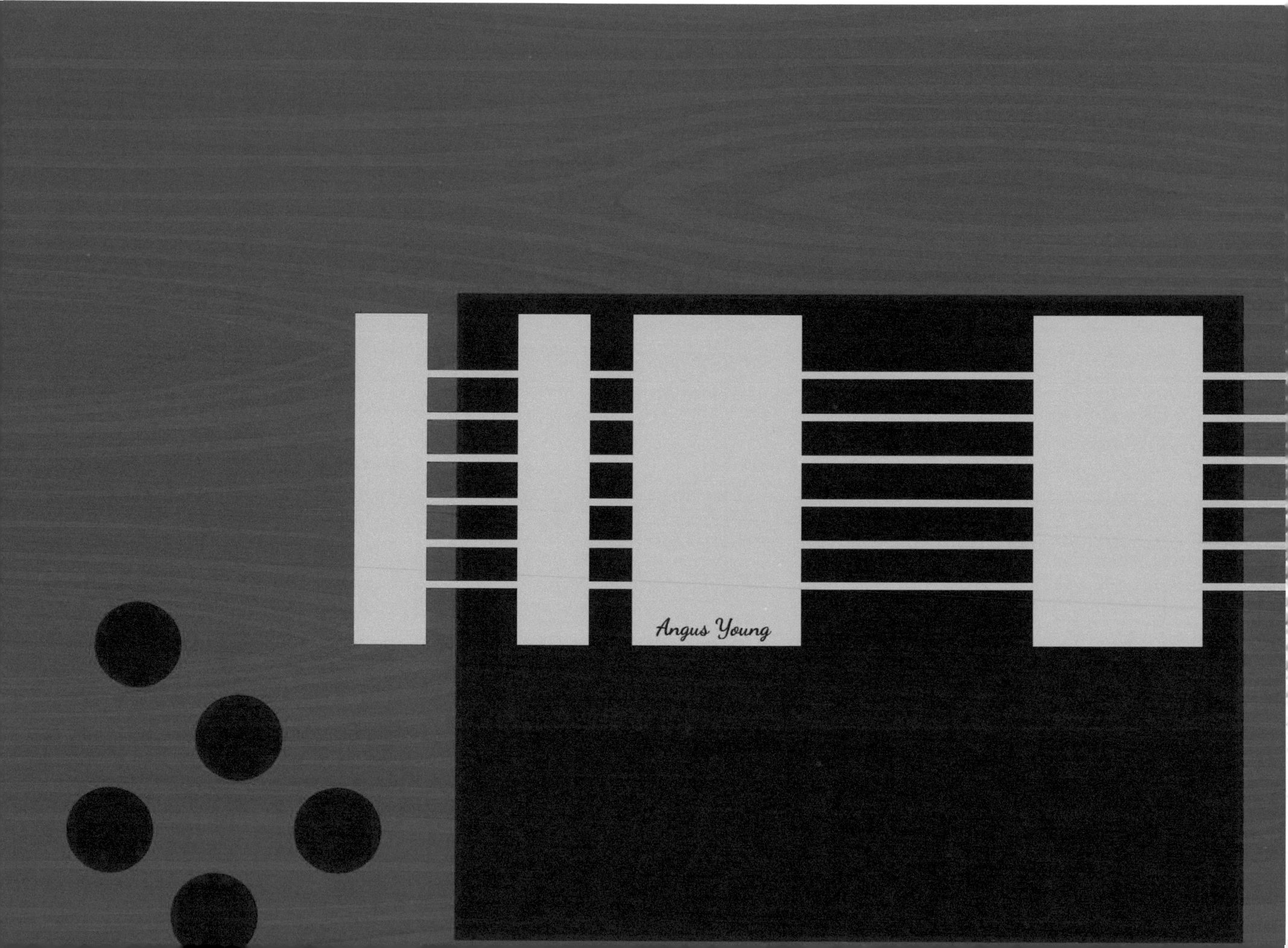

MARCH 2025

SUNDAY	MONDAY	TUESDAY	WEDNESDAY	THURSDAY	FRIDAY	SATURDAY
23	24	25	26	27	28	1
2	3	4	5 John Frusciante Born on this day 1970	6 David Gilmour Born on this day 1946	7	8
9	10	11	12	13	14	15
16	17 Billy Corgan Born on this day 1967	18	19 Billy Sheehan Born on this day 1953	20	21	22
23 Eric Clapton Born on this day 1945 30	24 Angus Young Born on this day 1955 31	25	26 James Iha Born on this day 1968	27	28	29

APRIL 2025

SUNDAY	MONDAY	TUESDAY	WEDNESDAY	THURSDAY	FRIDAY	SATURDAY
30	31	1	2	3	4	5
6	7	8	9	10 Warren Demartini Born on this day 1963	11	12
13	14	15	16	17	18	19
20	21	22	23 Steve Clark Born on this day 1960	24	25	26
27 Ace Frehley Born on this day 1951	28	29	30	1	2	3

MAY 2025

SUNDAY	MONDAY	TUESDAY	WEDNESDAY	THURSDAY	FRIDAY	SATURDAY
27	28	29	30	1	2 Link Wray Born on this day 1929	3
4 Dick Dale Born on this day 1937	5	6	7	8	9	10
11	12	13 Buckethead Born on this day 1969	14	15	16	17
18	19 Pete Townshend Born on this day 1945	20	21	22	23	24 Bob Dylan Born on this day 1941
25	26	27	28	29	30 Tom Morello Born on this day 1964	31

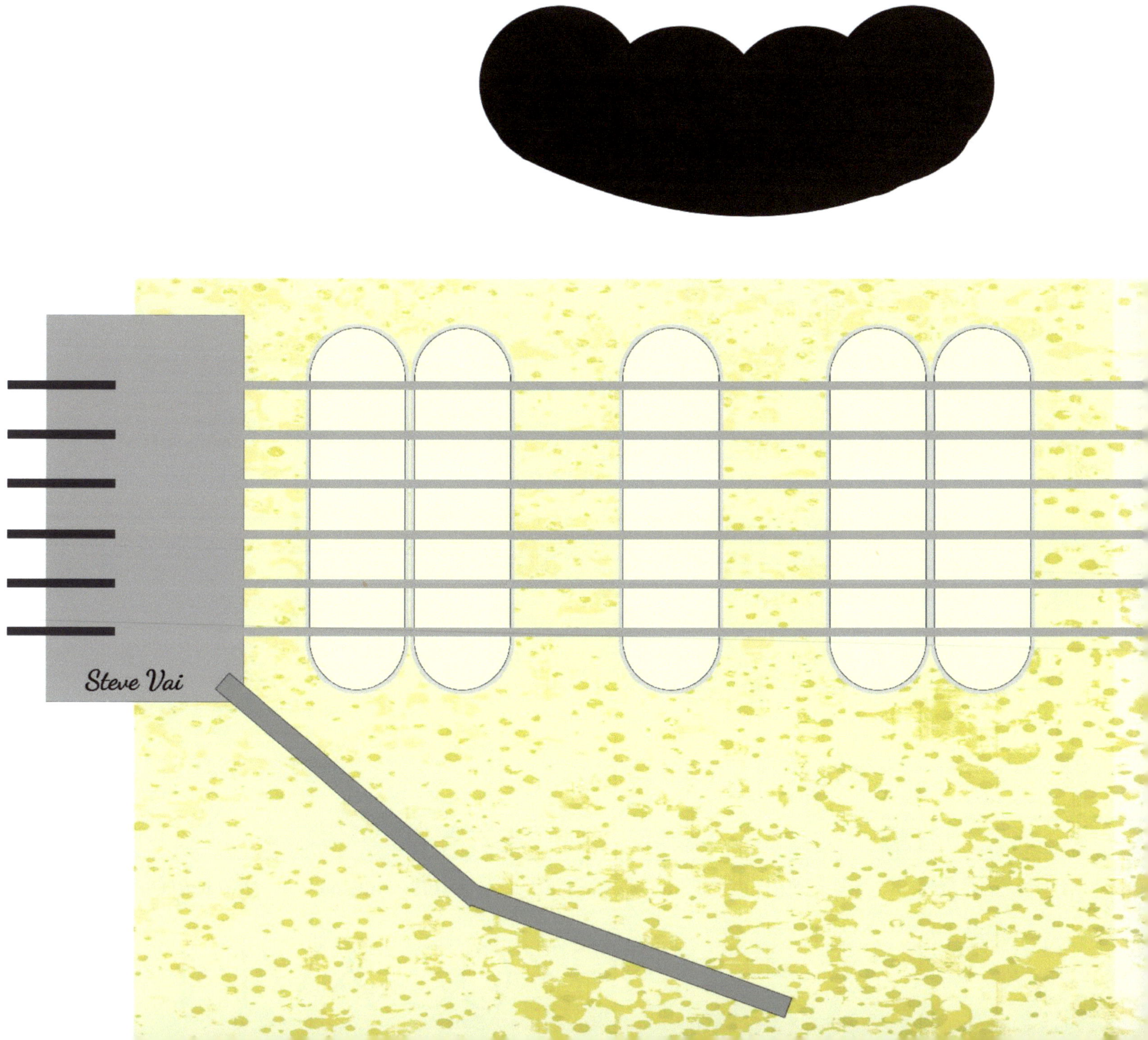

Steve Vai

JUNE 2025

SUNDAY	MONDAY	TUESDAY	WEDNESDAY	THURSDAY	FRIDAY	SATURDAY
1 Ronnie Wood Born on this day 1947	2	3	4	5	6 Steve Vai Born on this day 1960	7 Prince Born on this day 1958
8	9	10 Joey Santiago Born on this day 1965	11	12	13 Rivers Cuomo Born on this day 1970	14
15	16	17	18 Paul McCartney Born on this day 1942	19	20 Mike Anthony Born on this day 1954	21
22	23	24 Jeff Beck Born on this day 1944	25	26	27	28
29	30 Yngwie Malmsteen Born on this day 1963	1	2	3	4	5

JULY 2025

SUNDAY	MONDAY	TUESDAY	WEDNESDAY	THURSDAY	FRIDAY	SATURDAY
29	30	1	2	3	4	5
6	7	8 Toby Keith Born on this day 1961	9 Jack White Born on this day 1975	10	11	12
13	14	15 Joe Satriani Born on this day 1956	16	17 Geezer Butler Born on this day 1949	18	19 Brian May Born on this day 1947
20 Carlos Santana Born on this day 1947	21	22	23 Slash Born on this day 1965	24	25	26
27	28	29 Geddy Lee Born on this day 1953	30	31	1	2

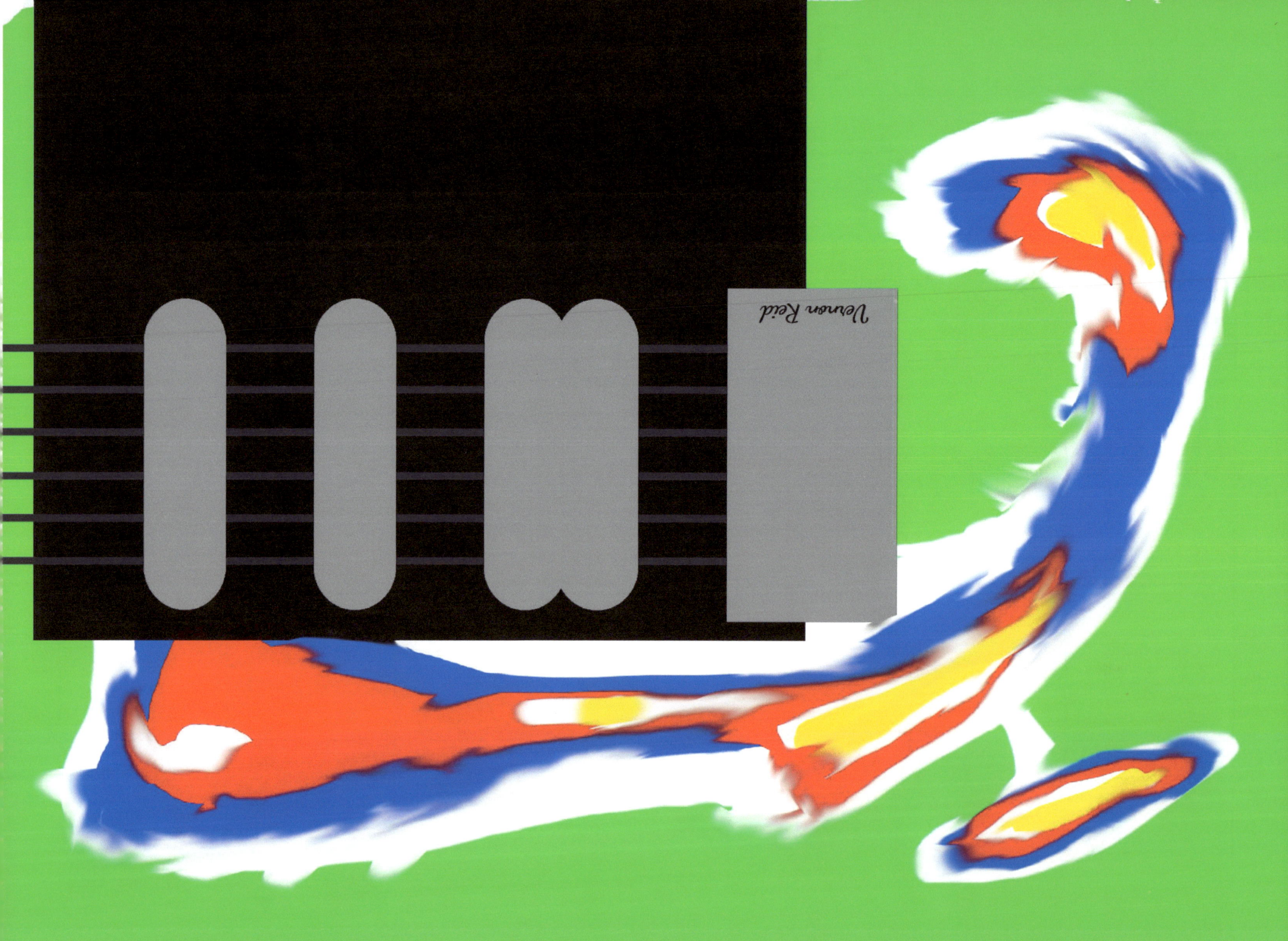

AUGUST 2025

SUNDAY	MONDAY	TUESDAY	WEDNESDAY	THURSDAY	FRIDAY	SATURDAY
27	28	29	30	31	1	2
3 James Hetfield Born on this day 1963	4	5	6	7	8 The Edge Born on this day 1961	9
10	11	12 Mark Knopfler Born on this day 1949	13	14	15	16
17	18	19	20 Dimebag Darrell Born on this day 1966	21	22 Vernon Reid Born on this day 1958	23
24 31	25	26	27 Alex Lifeson Born on this day 1953	28	29	30

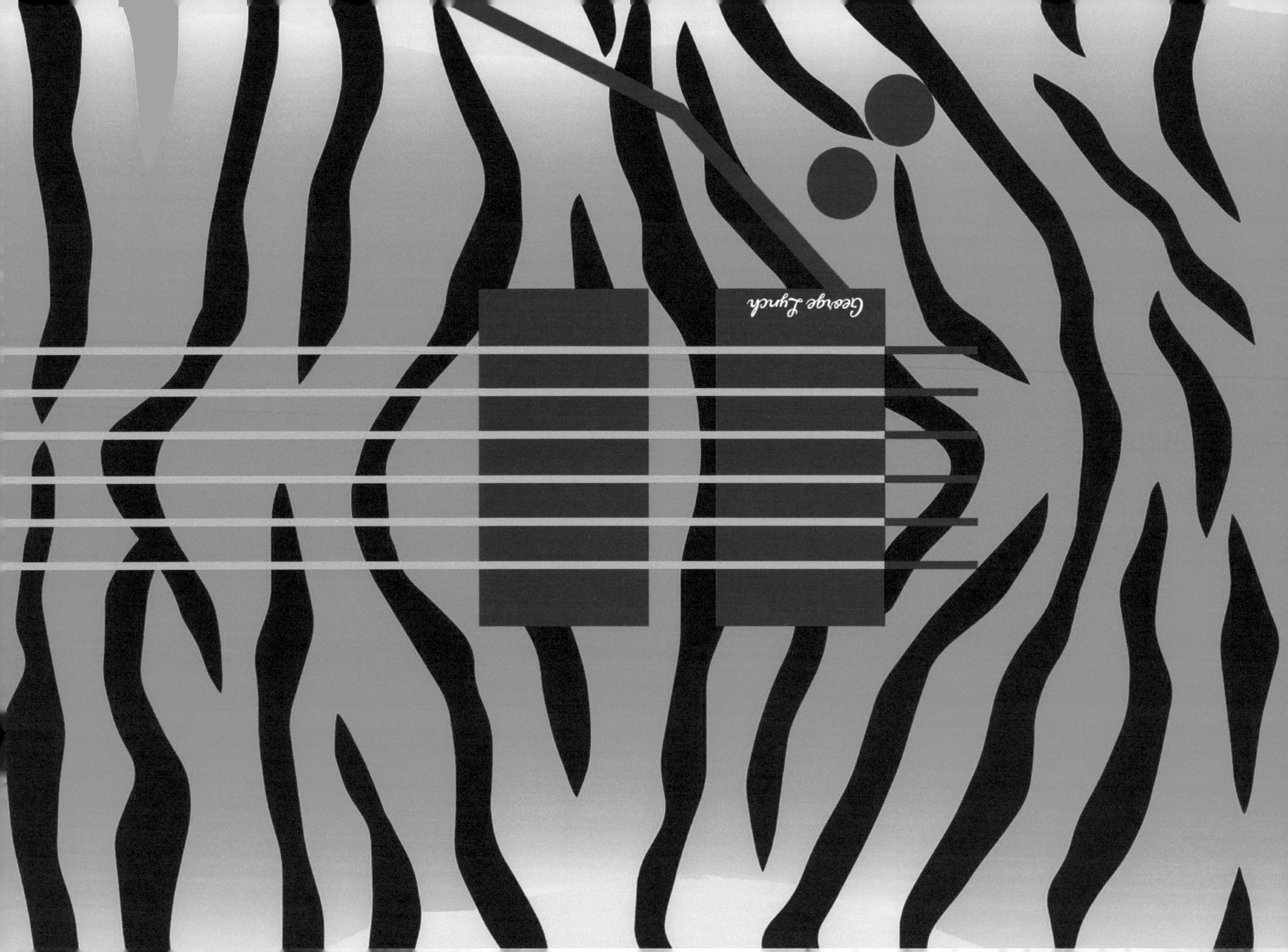

SEPTEMBER 2025

SUNDAY	MONDAY	TUESDAY	WEDNESDAY	THURSDAY	FRIDAY	SATURDAY
31	1	2	3 Steve Jones Born on this day 1955	4	5	6
7	8	9	10	11	12	13
14	15	16 BB King Born on this day 1925	17	18	19	20 Nuno Bettencourt Born on this day 1966
21	22	23 Bruce Springsteen Born on this day 1949	24	25	26	27
28 George Lynch Born on this day 1954	29 Les Claypool Born on this day 1963	30	1	2	3	4

OCTOBER 2025

SUNDAY	MONDAY	TUESDAY	WEDNESDAY	THURSDAY	FRIDAY	SATURDAY
28	29	30	1	2	3 Stevie Ray Vaughan Born on this day 1954	4
5	6	7	8 Johnny Ramone Born on this day 1948	9 John Entwistle Born on this day 1944 John Lennon Born on this day 1940	10	11
12	13 Sammy Hagar Born on this day 1947	14	15	16	17	18 Chuck Berry Born on this day 1926
19	20	21	22	23	24	25
26	27	28	29	30	31 Johnny Marr Born on this day 1963	1

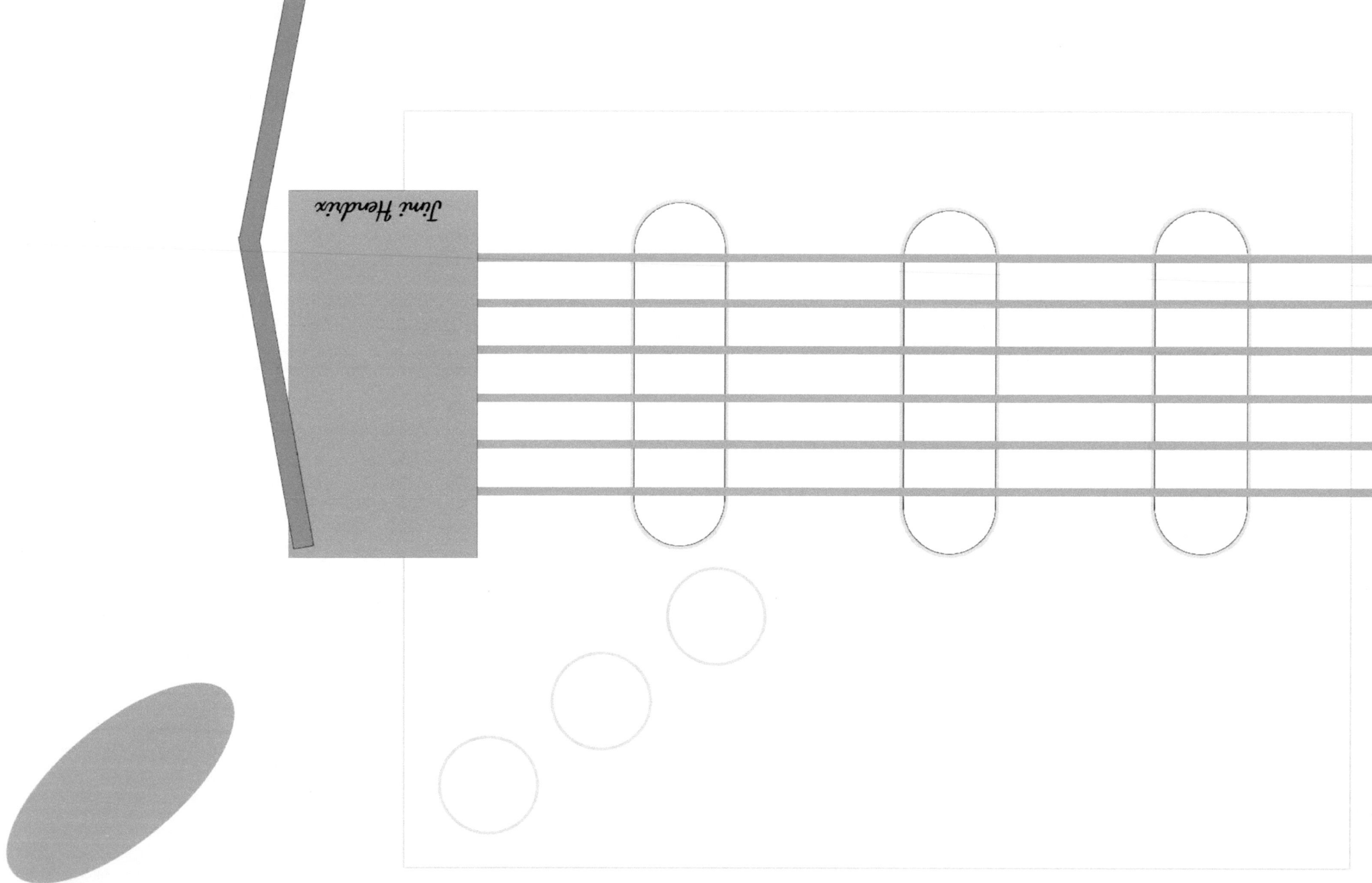

NOVEMBER 2025

SUNDAY	MONDAY	TUESDAY	WEDNESDAY	THURSDAY	FRIDAY	SATURDAY
26	27	28	29	30	31	1
2	3	4	5	6 Paul Gilbert Born on this day 1966	7	8
9	10	11	12	13	14	15
16	17	18 Kirk Hammett Born on this day 1962	19	20	21	22
23 / 30	24	25	26	27 Jimi Hendrix Born on this day 1942	28	29 John Mayall Born on this day 1933

DECEMBER 2025

SUNDAY	MONDAY	TUESDAY	WEDNESDAY	THURSDAY	FRIDAY	SATURDAY
30	1	2	3	4	5	6 Randy Rhoads Born on this day 1956
7	8	9	10	11	12	13 Tom Delonge Born on this day 1975
14	15	16	17	18 Keith Richards Born on this day 1943	19	20
21	22 Rick Nielsen Born on this day 1948	23	24	25 Jimmy Buffett Born on this day 1946	26	27
28	29	30	31	1	2	3

GUITAR MODELS RANKED

1 Fender Stratocaster
2 Gibson Les Paul
3 Fender Telecaster
4 Gibson SG
5 Gibson ES-335
6 Ibanez JEM
7 PRS Custom 24
8 Epiphone Les Paul
9 Gretsch White Falcon
10 Fender Jazzmaster
11 Gibson Explorer
12 Jackson Soloist
13 ESP LTD EC-1000
14 Rickenbacker 360
15 Gretsch Duo Jet
16 Gibson Flying V
17 Schecter C-1

18 Rickenbacker 330
19 Danelectro U2
20 Epiphone Casino
21 Music Man John Petrucci
22 Charvel San Dimas
23 Gretsch G5420T
24 PRS SE Custom 24
25 Ibanez RG Series
26 Jackson Dinky
27 Gibson Firebird
28 ESP Eclipse
29 Fender Mustang
30 PRS SE Santana
31 Danelectro 59DC
32 Ibanez RG550
33 Jackson Rhoads
34 Fender Jaguar

35 Gretsch Country Gentleman
36 Gibson SG Standard
37 PRS SE Standard 24
38 Gibson ES-175
39 Gibson Firebird V
40 Epiphone SG
41 Ibanez S Series
42 Gretsch G6136T
43 ESP LTD M Series
44 Gibson Nighthawk
45 Schecter Hellraiser C-1
46 Jackson King V
47 Dean ML
48 Epiphone Riviera
49 Yamaha Pacifica
50 Gibson ES-339

RICHEST GUITARISTS RANKED

1. Paul McCartney 1.2 Billion
2. Jimmy Buffett 600 Million
3. Bruce Springsteen 500 Million
4. Keith Richards 500 Million
5. Eric Clapton 450 Million
6. The Edge 400 Million
7. Bob Dylan 375 Million
8. Toby Keith 365 Million
9. Dave Grohl 320 Million
10 Dave Matthews 300 Million

11. James Hetfield 300 Million
12. Brian May 210 Million
13. Ronnie Wood 200 Million
14. Kirk Hammett 200 MIllion
15. David Gilmour 180 Million
16. Jimmy Page 180 MIllion
17. Angus Young 160 Million
18. Pete Townshend 150 Million
19. Tony Iommi 140 Million
20. Mark Knopfler 100 Million

(IN US DOLLARS)